Tales of a Seattle Mariners Groundskeeper

Living the Dream

Memoirs of the Most Fun Job I Ever Had

Rich Korb

Seattle Mariners Groundskeeper
1984 -1985

Dedicated to –

The 1984 – 1985 Grounds Crew for
the Seattle Mariners

Contents

About the Author

Rich Korb has been a junior high and high school coach. During his coaching experience he also played on city recreation teams. Rich had tryouts with the San Francisco 49ers and the Seattle Seahawks as a placekicker. He eventually got the opportunity to kick for a semi-pro football team. Those experiences allowed Rich to meet and become friends with professional athletes.

Rich has always enjoyed team sports as well as individual efforts which include riding his bicycle 1,860 miles over 29 days from Washington State to Wisconsin. His book and YouTube video - *The Bicycle Cowboy* - share his experiences and offers tips for bicycle touring.

Rich enjoys writing and sharing his life surrounding sports with others offering the challenge of catching your dreams.

Preface

I think most youngsters who play sports have had the dream of one day playing in the major leagues. I had that dream and the dream became a reality. In the words of Robert Griffin III after winning the Heisman Trophy Award, "Don't chase your dreams, catch them." I was presented with the opportunity to catch the dream of playing major league baseball.

During my undergraduate work with Dr. Foreman at Seattle Pacific University I took his class – Sports and Society. It was a life-changing experience for me. Our first assignment was to define – *play, game, sport and professional.* I found out that play is at the root of all levels of athletics. It is play that sparks our interest to move toward higher levels of competition. It is the joy we derive from play that fulfills our inner being.

Throughout the 1984 and 1985 seasons as a groundskeeper for the Seattle Mariners, I was granted the pleasure of playing with major league baseball players. I was able to play catch, hit, sit in the bullpen and eat with professional athletes. In Dr. Foreman's class I also learned the definition of a professional is one who is paid for what they do, and I did get paid. I had caught the dream of my youth.

This book is about the experiences and the joy of living that dream.

Acknowledgements

I want to thank the King County Maintenance Division for hiring me to serve as a groundskeeper. The position put me on the playing field with major league teams. It is through that opportunity I am able to bring the reader up close and personal with behind the scene and inside stories of major league baseball from my perspective.

I also want to acknowledge Larry O'Brien, a teaching colleague and friend for editing this book. Your insight in baseball and writing made this book come together. Without your help this project would not have gone forward with the flair it possesses. Thanks Larry.

Corky Trewin, photographer for the Seattle Mariners, graciously provided permission to use his photograph of the Kingdome from the 300 level as the cover for this book.

Introduction

My first experience with major league baseball was as a child at the Los Angeles Coliseum where the Los Angeles Dodgers played their games after moving from Brooklyn, New York. My father took me to two games. After the Dodgers moved into Dodger Stadium on April 27, 1962, my father took me to a Pirates game since he was from Pittsburgh. It was then that I began my journey into baseball.

We were living in Sierra Madre, California when I heard an announcement at school about Little League sign-ups. I needed a parent to sign me up, so I asked my father if he would. He did and I joined the Eagles as a pitcher.

The local Union 76 gas station handed out 8"x11" pictures of Dodger players. Collecting pictures and trading with friends was a big deal. The walls of my room were covered with pictures. I remember looking at those pictures and wondering if I had what it took to become a major league baseball player.

My friends and I were the sand lot kids and the neighbor's dog, located behind our backstop, ate many of our baseballs just like in the movie. From the swimming pool to the experiences of the film you could have put our faces on the actors and know what our early baseball experiences and youth were like.

Two years later my father took a job with Rocket Research in Huntsville, Alabama. I wondered what baseball was like in Alabama and was excited to play. Alabama had a tryout system where you played in the minor league or major league depending on ability. I remember showing up at practice one day and being told I was not allowed to play in the major league because my skills were not good enough. However, the coaches told me I could play in the minor league and sent me home. I remember crying all the way home. I figured my chances of playing baseball at the professional level were over.

Our family moved across town so I thought I could try playing over there. The new league also had tryouts, but this time I knew what to expect, so I bore down and got real serious. During the tryouts I focused on my hitting and began to hit reasonably well until I injured my foot running to first base where I twisted my ankle in a water run-off groove first baseline was placed on. I tore the ligaments in the bottom of my foot and needed therapy. My father never allowed me to play again after reading what a professional baseball player said about how bad little league baseball was for young arms.

Not being allowed to play, I made miniature baseball fields in the dirt of our backyard, basketball courts from scrap wood, and built a stadium for the electric football game in my bedroom and painted the teams.

When I was 14 a friend I had been playing city league basketball with asked me to tryout for his baseball team. I had not played organized baseball since I was 10. The transformation of skills during those off years was amazing for those who had stayed with the sport. They threw curve balls and could hit them as well. My skills were lacking. I never went back.

Fifteen years later I was coaching junior high baseball. During that time a substitute teacher told me about a position at the Kingdome as a groundskeeper. I learned that I would be constructing the baseball field for the Seattle Mariners which lead to hitting in the batting cage, getting hit by foul balls, messing around with players, driving out the cage, TV time, autograph courier for teachers, wild cats/kittens in the stadium, a Sports Illustrated photo and meeting famous baseball players.

All of what I had hoped for as a kid playing in Sierra Madre, California, and Huntsville, Alabama, was becoming a reality. I was on the field with major league baseball players and playing baseball.

Short Stories from the Dream

Preparing the Kingdome for Opening Day

On April 3, 1984, I entered the Kingdome with tremendous excitement and anticipation. I was a member of the Seattle Mariners Grounds Crew and standing on the playing surface of the NCAA Men's Final Four, Seattle Supersonics, Seattle Seahawks, and the Seattle Mariners.

The Kingdome was cavernous and dimly lit. Before me was the massive concrete floor with a lone lamp standing in the middle of this gigantic stadium. It was a leftover of the Seattle City Swap Meet. The King County Maintenance Department and the Grounds Crew were there to convert the Kingdome into a major league ballpark for the Opening Day game between the Seattle Mariners and the Toronto Blue Jays. We had 16 hours to have the stadium ready.

All Seattle sports teams leased the Kingdome from the county. When one team played in the Kingdome there could be no banners or signs publicizing another team. It was our job to make the stadium their home for game day.

The massive army of forklift drivers, and Zamboni operators, along with rolls of Astroturf, two kinds of dirt, dugouts, outfield walls, line paint and chalk began to convert the stadium into the stage for the Opening Day of America's greatest pastime.

Everyone worked on various aspects of the conversion. The grounds crew was primarily responsible for the playing surface. Great concentration and care were given to the preparation of the pitcher's mound as this was the main focus of the game. If something went wrong, such as the dirt not being packed properly or it started to come apart, the grounds crew would be on the center stage of television and all the fans at the game. Nobody wanted to be in that situation!

The pitcher's mound was brought in on a special tractor. The mound was suspended under the extended frame of the tractor by two chains which were connected to two eyebolts on either side of the mound. The eyebolts needed to be hidden with wet clay and tightly packed with packing stamps. Precision as to the placement between the pitching rubber and the back of home plate was essential. The height of the mound had to be precise as well as the diameter. All mounds were prepared the same way with special clay to create a solid bond for better footing. The batter's box was of the same clay. Sliding dust was added to the areas around the bases to create a better sliding surface. I often wondered what the umpires would do if they found a discrepancy in one of the dimensions of the field. Would they stop the game? Would they make the grounds crew fix it? I did not want to know the answer.

Each groundskeeper was put in charge of their own base area. The batter's box clay and the dirt surrounding the batter's box were controlled by the lead of the grounds crew. Members of the maintenance crew installed the Astroturf, painted the permanent lines, and positioned the dugouts, bull pens, backstop net, the outfield wall and all Opening Day Banners. It was a sight to behold when we were finished.

As we worked on that first day, I heard a scream from the Mariner's bullpen. I don't remember a woman being on the crew, but I know I heard a scream. Have you ever heard a man scream? Well it's just plain wrong to hear a man scream. I've tried to scream, just to see if I could physically do it. It's just not normal, but it is possible because I heard it and saw it. Startled I spun around to see what was happening. With all the machinery and commotion I figured someone might get hurt, and maybe this was the moment. Two maintenance crew members had been rolling out a piece of Astroturf, but now they were screaming as they stood looking at something on the ground. Always ready to help someone in distress I ran to them wondering as I ran – "What's going on?" I could not see anything to warrant such a commotion, but the one guy was still screaming when I got there. I looked down at what he was screaming about, and there on the Astroturf were five kittens that had been inside the roll of Astroturf. When the two maintenance crew members had unrolled the turf they discovered the kittens. These kittens were wild street kittens and were hissing with teeth and claws ready to put up a good fight. I have always appreciated animals and felt sorry that these kittens had been brought into the stadium against their wishes and without their mother. The maintenance crew members tried to discourage me from picking up the kittens and wanted to destroy them on the spot, but wearing leather gloves and securing a cardboard box, I picked up each kitten and placed it in the box. Each one clawed and bit as soon as I attempted to pick them up.

I came to discover during a later game that the Kingdome was of full wild street cats, and the mothers usually gave birth inside the cardboard cylinders that the Astroturf was rolled onto. One cat got onto the field during a game later in the season, but that too is a story later in the book.

I had never heard a man scream until that night. The maintenance worker was harassed to no end about his screaming. There was an offer made that if he could scream the maintenance department would not mention it again. Wanting to end his misery, he tried desperately to scream, but nothing would come out. It's amazing what the human brain can do under extreme stress.

As the night wore on, the maintenance and grounds crew were provided a full course meal in the stadium kitchen and dining area. I don't think I ever had dinner at 2a.m. until that day.

Night had turned to day and it was now April 4, 1984. Opening Day for the new season had arrived. Media, players and coaches began to show up as morning turned into afternoon. Three of us who were working on the pitcher's mound suddenly we were engulfed in a bright light. While looking down, I told the other two groundskeepers, "Don't look up if you want to be on TV." We didn't and later that day a local special was presented to the community showing a series of videos about how the Kingdome had been converted from a concrete tomb into a major league baseball field prepared for Opening Day, including the three of us on the mound.

This was the beginning of a new era for me. When I returned to teaching after spring break I was inundated with requests from students and staff who had seen me on TV. I was unprepared for this volume of requests to get autographs and tickets for students and staff.

Getting My Major League Cap from the Mariner's Uniform Locker

A most memorable and unexpected event took place on my first day suiting up in a grounds crew uniform. I was escorted to the Mariner's clubhouse by another grounds crew member. We walked in and there were all the Mariners getting suited up for the game. It was like we were part of the team. We entered the uniform locker and I was asked by the uniform manager what my head size was. He promptly handed me an official Mariner's major league cap and informed me that this cap was free. If I lost it I would have to pay for the next one. I will never forget that moment. I had received team caps from coaches I had played for as a kid, and that was special because I felt like I was part of the team. However, this experience was exceptional. I never could have predicted that I would be in a major league clubhouse wearing the teams cap. When I left the uniform locker, I was wearing a

Seattle Mariners major league baseball cap just like the major league baseball players in the clubhouse.

Joe DiMaggio Providing Two Autographed Baseballs

As I entered the locker room for the Kingdome ushers and groundskeepers, Scotty quickly and quietly told me, "Get your pen and two brand new baseballs ready." "Who's in town?" I asked. "Mr. Coffee! You know – Joe DiMaggio!" Scotty stated in excitement. Wow! Joe DiMaggio! I instantly began to think of who would give anything to get an autograph from one of the greatest baseball players of all time.

I quickly got my uniform on and acquired two brand new baseballs and a new pen. There could be no mistakes if I was to get an autograph on the first attempt. There would not be a second opportunity. This was a once in a lifetime chance.

Scurrying out the locker room door like a rat leaving the nest, I entered the stadium under the first baseline bleachers. It was dark with shafts of light knifing through the seams in the bleacher floor. I could hear people moving and talking above me as they found their seats. I wondered if they knew who was in the stadium that night.

Eagerly creeping along between the bleacher's steel support post and the concrete wall, I could see the entrance to the visiting team's dugout. My heart was pounding with anticipation as I formulated a plan of how I would approach Mr. DiMaggio. To insure the best chance for an autograph, I always address a celebrity humbly with honor and respect. This approach only failed once, but that is another amazing story.

Approaching the dugout doorway, I observed a large entourage of media coming from the Mariner's dugout. They were coming directly toward me. I was the only one in the visiting team's dugout and in plain view of the group heading my way. The media was providing more space for Mr.

DiMaggio's group than the usual, which is more like a feeding frenzy. I told myself, "Stay cool and calm. Keep your mind clear. Demonstrate honor yet show intent and a little eagerness. You are going to address the greatest baseball player in Seattle on this night. Make sure you project that to Mr. DiMaggio."

Our eyes met. I gave Mr. DiMaggio the customary male to male honor glance and stepped aside allowing him to move to his destination. Low and behold he sat down in the visiting team's dugout. Mr. DiMaggio was right in front of me. The media formed a half circle five yards away from Mr. DiMaggio. Only his escorts sat near, not next to, Mr. DiMaggio. This was an impromptu news conference, and I was standing in the middle of the media circle directly in front of Mr. DiMaggio. No member of the media blasted questions. They only spoke to Mr. DiMaggio when he pointed at them after they had raised their hand. I had never seen such control of the media nor have I since. He was in complete control.

Deciding my best chance to get the autographs was to humbly hold the baseballs and pen at just below chest height making sure of my intent and that all the necessary supplies were visible. I did not want to embarrass myself or Mr. DiMaggio. I found it interesting that the media was not taking pictures. I suspect they were a selected elite group with clear expectations of their behavior while in Mr. DiMaggio's presence.

With a nod of his head, as a king to a subject, Mr. DiMaggio indicated for me to approach his throne, a throne he had occupied for many years throughout his illustrious career. I had to wonder what his thoughts were as he sat in that dugout as an advertising spokesman for Mr. Coffee. I slowly and humbly approached Mr. DiMaggio and extended one baseball, not wanting to appear presumptuous, and the pen. There is a sweet spot between the baseball laces where baseball players sign their names. Mr. DiMaggio turned the baseball to the correct spot and signed the baseball and handed it back to me then he motioned for the other ball. Mr.

DiMaggio signed the second ball and handed it back to me as well. What I found amazing during this exchange was that he continued to answer the media's questions while he signed two baseballs. Mr. DiMaggio handled himself as smoothly as if he was catching a fly ball on the run while contemplating how he was going to throw a guy out after he caught the ball. I said, "Thank you Mr. DiMaggio." He smiled and I slowly exited out of the dugout. I had accomplished what no other person on staff that night could do.

I deliberately and cautiously made my way back under the bleachers toward the locker room door. I knew there would not be ushers or grounds crew around, however knowing that did not hinder my deliberate intention of hiding the baseballs deep within my locker and behind clothing. I took just as much caution when I exited the Kingdome with the two baseballs as I moved into the dark of the night well after the game was over.

Arriving at home that night I thought of who I could give the baseballs to. The value of a signed baseball given to someone who appreciated it is invaluable.

At that time I was teaching and coaching at Finn Hill Junior High School and working with an English teacher who was a virtual baseball encyclopedia. He could provide names, stats and facts of any player from any year. He had an amazing memory. His brother could do the same thing with rock and roll. Retrieving a Christmas label and some ribbon I wrote, "Jim - Christmas comes early once in a lifetime and this one is for you."

The following day I got to school early and placed a Joe DiMaggio autographed baseball in the dark recesses of Jim's mailbox to avoid detection. When I went to the locker room I decided to leave the building door unlocked as well as the locker room door, as I knew Jim would break down the doors to ask me about the baseball and the autograph. I do believe in divine appointments and this one was for Jim and me.

Jim came through the doors hollering, "Rich! Rich!" I was in the towel room when he came in. He wanted to know if the autograph was really Joe DiMaggio's. When I said yes and told him this story tears came to his eyes. Watching an adult become a child again is special, and I was able to do that for many people, mostly the female teachers. They seem to have this thing about athletes. But that is also another story. Oh, the other baseball went to the athletic director Stan to add to his sports memorabilia collection.

When Joe DiMaggio passed away, people told me I was a fool for giving away the baseballs. They said, "You could have retired and been worth millions." But the monetary value of two autographed baseball signed by Joe DiMaggio could not match the joy I felt in making my friends happy with a once in a lifetime gift.

The 1984 Detroit Tiger's Consecutive on the Road Winning Streak Record Attempt Ended with a Seattle Mariners Groundskeeper Touching a Fair Ball

The Detroit Tigers were riding high with one of the best on the road consecutive winning records in American League history. They had won 17 straight on the road wins and were one win away from breaking the record until . . . .

The landslide toward the Seattle Mariners defeating the Detroit Tigers on May 25, 1984 began when a groundskeeper sitting in the Tiger's dugout touched a fair ball.

Gene Guidi, Detroit Free Press sportswriter, wrote, "With one out in the first, the Tiger right-hander hit Barry Bonnell with a pitch and then gave up a run-scoring double down the left-field line to Seattle's hot hitting rookie first baseman, Alvin Davis." What happened to the ball hit by Alvin

Davis, down the left-field line, is the rest of the story.

Two groundskeepers had been assigned to the Tiger's third baseline bullpen. During the first inning with a runner on first base and the two groundskeepers not paying attention to the game, the next batter hit a hard grounder which landed just inches inside third base and hooked sharply outside the foul line. By the time the groundskeepers saw the ball it was in foul territory and heading very fast toward the bull pen. The whole Tiger's bullpen started running down the wall toward the Mariner's dugout to get away from the fair ball while one of the groundskeepers grabbed his chair and headed toward left field to escape the fast approaching grounder. It is customary for someone in the bullpen to grab balls in foul territory and pass them to the ball girl to give to an appreciative fan. The remaining groundskeeper realized he was the only one sitting on the bench and bent down to pick-up the ball, and noticing that the left fielder was charging hard toward the bullpen, he realized the ball must be fair. The groundskeeper saw that the ball was now in flight after launching off the bullpen mound and was heading straight toward him. He turned sideways hoping to avoid being hit by the fair ball and tried to stay out of the left fielder's way. Although the groundskeeper's plan was honorable, the ball hit him and went under the bench. He froze in his position, hoping not to cause any more trouble as the left fielder picked up the ball from under the bench and threw the ball to the shortstop. In the meantime the Seattle runner, who had been on first, had safely made it to second and was rounding toward third while the batter was arriving at first base. The rules state that when a fair ball is touched by a non-player, at that moment the play is over and any runners are awarded the next base plus one. Well that put the lead runner at home plate for the Mariner's first score and Alvin Davis at second base.

Thinking that the melee was over as the other groundskeeper returned to his seat and the Tiger's bullpen returned to their seats, Sparky

Anderson, the Tiger's manager came out of the dugout. He marched toward the second base umpire and started to have a heated discussion. Then to the embarrassment of the groundskeeper who touched the ball, Sparky Anderson stepped aside of the umpire and pointed at the groundskeeper. His action promptly caused the whole Tiger bullpen to start making comments to the groundskeeper. Finally a relief pitcher, 6'6'' Glenn Abbott, got up and walked over to the groundskeeper and said, "Do you know the rules of baseball?" Not realizing that the groundskeeper went to the same church as Glenn, and had also played basketball with him, looked Glenn straight in the eye, and said, "Hi. Glenn." Realizing he knew the groundskeeper, Glenn returned to his seat without another word from anyone. The inning closed with the Mariners leading 1-0, and the groundskeeper quickly heading toward the Mariner's dugout refusing to return to the Tiger's bullpen.

My action as the groundskeeper who touched a fair ball brought about the first run for the Mariners to beat the Tigers 7-3 and stopped the Tiger's quest for a new American League on the road consecutive wins record.

Fourteen year later while driving for Swift Transportation on a delivery to Detroit I heard warehouse personnel discussing a sports announcer's comments about the potential record breaking game being lost due to a groundskeeper touching a fair ball. When I told them the full story they were fascinated and angry.

I never thought I would be responsible for scoring a run in the Major Leagues, especially one that would alter the history for the World Championship Tigers who went on to win the World Series that year. And that is the rest of the story.

http://archive.freep.com/article/20140525/SPORTS02/30 5250096/detroit-tigers-flashback-1984-seattle-mariners

Billy Martin Attacked by a Drunken Fan and Dave Winfield's Support

The immortal New York Yankees were in Seattle for a three-game series in 1985. Billy Martin had just replaced Yogi Berra as manager and was under severe scrutiny by Yankees' Owner George Steinbrenner, team management, the media and the fan base. I remember hearing hecklers and seeing marshmallows flying onto the field in response to Billie punching a marshmallow salesman. During the game a drunken fan climbed over the camera pit fence and onto the third baseline side of the field. I thought Billy Martin was in real trouble.

Billy Martin had taken over coaching third base, and the Yankees were at bat when out of the stands came a small drunk man in a red shirt and blue jeans heading toward Billy. Billy's back was turned to the stands when the home plate umpire stopped the game. I was in the Yankees' dugout doorway. Dave Winfield was in the on deck circle. When Billy turned around and saw the drunken fan approaching him from maybe 30' away, Billy began to slowly walk down third baseline heading toward home plate.

Things got interesting when the 6'6", 220 pound Dave Winfield adjusted his batting helmet while holding his bat with the other hand and began to slowly walk toward Billy Martin with the drunk fan yelling and taunting Billy. As Billy Martin passed Dave Winfield, Dave Winfield positioned himself between Billy and the drunk. The drunk was a short man and walked right into Dave Winfield's stomach. The drunk's head met a towering Dave Winfield who was peering down at him. The drunken fan began to back away and Dave Winfield just kept backing the guy up while Dave slowly swung his bat in small circles as if he was going to hit the guy. At that point police and security personnel entered the field and took the drunk away.

The entertainment was topped off with the Mariners' winning the game.

I will always remember the final night Yogi Berra managed the Yankees in Seattle. I was behind the Yankees' dugout along the dark pathway that led to the groundskeeper's locker room. Yogi Berra was standing in the dugout door watching the game. I knew I was watching a legend of the game. I had grown up watching him catch for the New York Yankees. Now I was alone with this icon of major league baseball. I stood there admiring his profile of 5'7" with a protruding belly and thinking about all that he was and meant to baseball. He was wearing leather cleats with steel spikes. The leather was polished and cracking. They looked like a pair he had played in. I will never forget that profile. It was a special moment for me, one that I wanted to keep for myself. This was a childhood dream come true. I could have asked him for an autograph, and I'm sure he would have obliged, but what meant more to me was the memory. He might have been short in stature, yet he was a mountain of a man to those privileged to have met him.

Reggie Jackson Declining Autograph

Four of us groundskeepers sat in the Angels dugout prior to the game. The Angels' were in town with Rod Carew and Reggie Jackson who were closing out their major league careers. No Hollywood script writer could have created what would unfold that night.

As the four of us sat in the dugout, Reggie Jackson was finishing up his pregame fielding drills and was headed toward us. I told the fellas I was going to asked Reggie Jackson for an autograph. They all laughed and said, "You will never get an autograph from Reggie Jackson." "Why not?" I asked. "Because you're white," they responded. "He never gives white people autographs."

As Reggie Jackson walked past us, I stood up with baseball and pen in hand and said, "Excuse me Mr. Jackson. Could I get your autograph?" He just looked at me, shook his head no, and walked to the clubhouse. I couldn't believe it. I was shocked, so I decided to make it my personal mission that night to let Reggie Jackson know I didn't care about skin color and he shouldn't either.

During the game I made several attempts to get Reggie's attention. I thought if I was humble and polite he might soften. I had conceded the autograph, so I would settle for a simple friendly acknowledgement. Just a smile, a hello and a head nod would do. I would increase the stakes until he conceded.

Reggie Jackson did not sit with the team on the bench. He was the designated hitter and spent his time in the clubhouse watching the game while waiting to bat. I knew that I could intercept him between the dugout and the clubhouse by painting the bases (which was a requirement for the seventh inning base change) behind the Angels' dugout. I also knew that nobody else would be at the intercept point. Reggie would not be put on the spot, and nobody would know that he had been cordial to a white groundskeeper. As Reggie Jackson left the dugout and headed to the clubhouse our eyes met. I said, "Hi." He just looked away and walked past.

Later in the game Reggie was standing in the dugout door waiting to bat. He kept his bats crisscrossed and placed against the bleacher wall behind the dugout. This was perfect! I figured if I took one of his bats and took a couple of swings he had to say something. So while standing approximately 15' away from Reggie Jackson I took one of his bats and began to swing it. I was watching to see what he would do. Reggie moved his right arm in a backward motion with his palm open indicating for me to place the bat in his hand. I thought to myself, "No way am I going to give him his bat." I simply placed it in the stack with his other bats and just stood there.

My final attempt came later in the game when Reggie Jackson visited the media bathroom behind the dugout. When Reggie entered the bathroom I followed him in. As I left the bathroom and took up my position in the dugout door. I thought for sure he would say something. He did not even look at me.

When the game ended and the grounds crew was cleaning up the dugouts and watering the field, a fight broke out in the Angel's clubhouse. Players and managers were yelling and things were being knocked over. The high school clubhouse boys came running out the door with anxious looks on their faces. Several of us on the grounds crew asked what was going on. They said, "Reggie Jackson and Rod Carew got into a fight and players had to break them apart." "What caused the fight?" we asked. One of the clubhouse boys reported, "Reggie was getting after the clubhouse manager about the food and was questioning why there was not seafood since Seattle was the seafood capital of the country. Rod Carew came to the aid of the clubhouse manager at which Reggie took offense, and took a swing at Rod. The fight was on and players and managers had to break it up."

The clubhouse manager was white. I hope Reggie came to find the value in all people. After all, it's not the color of the skin but the nature of one's soul.

Lou Piniella's Journey to Seattle Begins

In 1985 Lou Piniella was also in his final season as a major league baseball player, but Lou was not through with baseball. During his final stop in Seattle, during the 1985 season, Lou was looking for a management position.

As batting practice came to a close and the grounds crew was taking the batting practice equipment off the field, I was driving the batting cage between second and third base on my way to the outfield storage area. Lou Piniella was standing in my path as I drove the John Deere tractor with the batting cage in tow. It was policy that if a player needed anything, it was our responsibility to address and resolve their need. During this encounter, Lou placed his hand on the engine cowling of the tractor indicating that he wanted to me to stop. I stopped the tractor and Lou began to inquisitively look around the stadium while asking, "Is this all the fans you get here?" I looked around just as he had, looked him straight in the eye and said, "Well, Lou, it all depends on who we are playing." I will never forget his face. Something clicked in his expression. You know that kind of look when you know you have connected with a person's soul. Well I can't be sure what happened in Lou's head that night, but what I can tell you is that he had his longest stay as a manager with the Seattle Mariners, and was well loved by the community and his players.

I believe he saw the need expressed in those words I shared and made it his mission to become the manager of the Seattle Mariners. You're welcome Seattle. If I helped bring Lou Piniella to Seattle in 1993, then that fateful meeting at second base was worth it. Only Lou can tell us.

Jack Perconte's Shoe Gift and His Check Swing Off My Ankle

One of the benefits of being a groundskeeper is obtaining memorabilia from players. Jack Perconte was playing second base for the Seattle Mariners. Jack Perconte and I were about the same size, so I asked him for a pair of his shoes. At the time it was customary among the grounds crew to ask players for their shoes because the shoes matched our uniforms. Most players had shoe endorsements and getting shoes was not a problem.

On this particular night I was standing in the third baseline dugout door visiting with the head of the grounds crew. Jack was batting and he batted left handed. I knew that any checked swing or foul ball had the potential to end up in the dugout, so I moved my body just behind the Mariner's dugout door. Unfortunately, I left my right foot sticking out into the doorway opening when all of a sudden I felt this sharp pain shoot up my leg, the same feeling you get when you break a bone. Before I could sit down, the team trainer had left his post on the bench and was attending to my foot. When he pulled down my sock, my ankle had already swollen and the image of the baseball laces was imprinted on my ankle. Jack had checked his swing while catching a piece of the ball and sent it like a bullet right into my ankle.

I took home a special memory from Jack Perconte that night along with his shoes. Thanks Jack.

Alvin Davis and Finn Hill Junior High

Special relationships develop between players and groundskeepers. The players know the effort groundskeepers put into making sure the field and player's needs are secured. It is through those understandings meaningful opportunities develop.

Alvin Davis was one of those special people I got to know on a personal level. Players in the major leagues are allotted tickets to games. Several times I was able to acquire tickets from various players. It was special when I could identify individuals I knew could not afford to attend a game and get them tickets.

While I was teaching physical education and coaching at Finn Hill Junior High School I had developed a program called Reach Out Club. The purpose of the club was to get students connected with students from other schools while going on outings together. Since Alvin Davis, as most professional athletes, was involved in community events I invited him to our school.

Alvin Davis Night was the promotion. He came to the school the afternoon before a home game to speak with the students about his journey to the major leagues and life's challenges. It was great for the students to see Alvin up close and listen to him speak and then to watch him on the field.

PTL and Sunflower Seeds

Alvin Davis and Jim Presley held down the corners at first and third base during the 1984 season. They were very devoted about their faith and did not hide it when speaking. Several of us on the grounds crew shared the same faith, so it became a custom when cleaning up their base just prior the first pitch to turn our broom upside down and write PTL in the dirt. PTL – "Praise the Lord" was a common statement of faith in the mid-80s. Jim Presley and Alvin Davis knew who prepared their base and would look over to us and point to the sky in acknowledgement of our secret statement.

Jim Presley was a jokester and chewed a lot of sunflower seeds. He was always looking for ways to embarrass me. One night just as the first pitch was to be thrown Jim called for time. He knew I was in the Mariner's dugout and asked the third base umpire to have the area around his base cleared of the sunflower seeds left over from batting practice. I retrieved the small hand pushed Zamboni and went onto the field to clean up third base. While I was cleaning the area, making sure not to look up as I worked, I asked Jim what was the problem with a few sunflower seeds. He said they fly up on ground balls and make it hard to field the ball.

Every time after that night when I cleaned his base prior to the start of the game I would write PTL in the dirt and leave a small pile of sunflower seeds on the base. Jim would kick the sunflower seeds off the bag and point at me.

Mike Stanton Beer Spill and Pouting

The bullpen pitching staff and I were heading to the Mariner's bullpen when from the stands I heard a disgruntled fan yell at Mike Stanton, "Hey Stanton! Why don't you go back to Calgary where you belong?" The Calgary Cannons were the Mariner's AAA farm team from 1985-1994. Mike did not look toward the stands, but maintained a steady course as we walked to the bullpen.

I arrived ahead of Mike Stanton and took up a seat to the left of the Gatorade container. I knew that was Mike's seat, I but thought I'd give it a shot to see what he'd do. Mike stood directly in front of me and motioned for me to move. During those days of the Kingdome, players sitting in the bull pen had their heads at the foot level of the fans who sat on the other side of the fence. I moved to the end of the bench and Mike took up his spot. Just as he sat down, beer spilled from a fans cup running down the back of Mike uniform making a large stain. I'm not sure how that happened, but I do know that no apology was given. Mike Stanton was red hot. He stayed cool, but he was clearly upset.

Later in the game Mike was called on to pitch. He went into the game, pitched to one batter and then was removed. I heard several of the pitchers in the bull pen say, "Watch out." I keyed in on the transfer of the ball to the pitching coach. Mike did not want to give up the ball, but the coach gestured twice until Mike forced the ball into the coach's hand and briskly walked off the mound heading toward the Mariner's dugout. As he walked across the field boos broke out. Mike did not stop in the dugout, but went straight into the clubhouse.

On another night when I was working in the Mariner's dugout, Mike was again pulled out of the game. I remembered what the players had said about watching out. As Mike Stanton walked toward the dugout, the lead groundskeeper said, "Get out of the way!" and directed me to follow him away from the dugout door. When Mike entered the club house I remember hearing a lot of yelling and equipment being thrown around.

Later that season the Mariners had a large 4'x 8' mirror installed in the staging area behind the dugout where players could work on their hitting and form. One night I noticed a sign had been posted on the mirror which read, "You break it. You buy it. $5,000." I wonder who that sign was for.

As the season progressed, I found myself working behind the Mariner's dugout more and more. There seemed to be more action and drama down there.

Players Hiding Behind the Dugout During the Singing of the National Anthem

Singing the national anthem is a tradition at all sporting events from youth sports to the big leagues. When a Canadian team came to Seattle the national anthem was sung for both countries. Players probably get tired of standing night after night after night holding their hats and waiting for the song to end. I can understand having stood through my share of anthem renditions. Often I would see players exciting the dugout as the singer was about to begin singing. This exodus happened most often when two anthems were going to be sung.

What I found most interesting about the exodus was how fast players would reappear at the dugout door if there was an exceptional singer or a young child singing, and bringing the house down with applause for their rendition of the song.

Umpire Stopped Game and Instructed Me to Get the Police to Remove a Heckler

Sitting in the bullpen can put you on the spot. Sometimes the grounds crew becomes the target of fan abuse. Other times you are called on to address the needs of umpires who have a reason to call timeout.

On this particular night I was working in the Mariner's bullpen when all of a sudden the game came to an abrupt halt. I started scanning around the stadium looking for what might have caused the game to stop. As I was looking around, the pitchers in the bullpen began to move away from me saying, "He wants you. You are in trouble." I thought, he? Who is he? Trouble? Why am I in trouble? It all became crystal clear when I looked toward home plate and the first base umpire was pointing straight at me and gesturing for me to come to him.

It was one of our duties to assist anyone associated with the game, so I made a brisk walk to the umpire. He said, "Don't look, but I want a uniformed police officer in the aisle next the camera pit as soon as the inning is over. A fan is throwing candy at me and needs to be ejected from the stadium. I will show the police officer which fan they need to deal with." I confirmed that I understood and made my way to the Mariner's dugout.

I found Wilbur, the lead groundskeeper sitting on his usual bucket just inside the dugout door. I told him what the umpire had requested. Wilbur quickly called for a police officer to come to our location. When the police arrived, I informed them of what the umpire had requested. Wilbur told me to return to the bullpen when the inning was over.

On my way back to the bullpen, I saw the same policeman I had spoken to standing in the aisle just above the camera pit. The umpire walked over to the fence and pointed out the heckler. The police quickly moved in and took the fan away. Later that night I was told by another groundskeeper the police had taken the fan to an office and issued him a fine and escorted him out of the stadium with a lifetime ban from any Mariner's game.

When I sat down in the bullpen, all the players who had moved away from me earlier were now sliding toward me and asking for information like junior high students looking for gossip.

I discovered that these bullpen pitchers were not much different than the junior high students I was teaching at the time. When they were not pitching, they goofed around and made silly comments just like the kids. However, when the phone rang asking for another pitcher, everybody got serious.

Phil Niekro Autograph

Being a physical education teacher in a junior high school has its challenges with young adolescents, but sometimes teachers can be just as challenging, especially when famous baseball players came to town. On this particular night the Seattle Mariners where playing the New York Yankees and "Knucksie" Phil Niekro, the famous knuckleball pitcher, was in town. I thought I was going to need to hold a lottery for an autograph. Fortunately Trudy, an English teacher who was mesmerized by athletes' physiques, especially famous ones, was the only one who asked for Phil Niekro's autograph.

Phil Niekro was a gentleman and made you feel welcome when you spoke to him. He gave you his full attention as if there was nobody else but you in the stadium. I always told athletes who the autograph was for. This created a special impression on the athlete knowing that I was on the grounds crew and was making a special effort to do for someone what they could not do for themselves. Most athletes understood their role and obliged with gratitude. Phil Niekro was one of those people.

Phil's knuckleball was very difficult to catch or block. I will never forget watching the catcher wearing an oversized glove painted bright orange. It was especially entertaining to watch the catcher's glove move around while wondering where the ball was going to cross the plate. Not even Phil knew where the ball was going to go. However, it was always close to the strike zone. I'm sure if umpires told their side of the knuckleball story, they too made a guess from time to time as to whether the pitch was a strike or a ball.

Sleeping In The Training Room

Teaching physical education all day after riding my bicycle 10 miles to school and then 10 miles home caused me to get fairly tired. When the Mariners had a home series, it became necessary to be at the

Kingdome by 5:30p.m.. Most of the games ended around 10:00, but sometimes extra innings were needed to determine a winner. When back to back series were played, teaching all day and working games at night became taxing on my energy levels. Sleeping in the school training room during lunch and planning period became a great option for catching up on sleep. The looks on some of the students' faces were interesting when I would stumble out the training room half asleep.

Church Before Sunday Games

One Sunday morning as we prepared the field for the day's game, I was walking through the media area directly behind home plate. I had always noticed a door that was marked "Media". On this particular day, the door was ajar. I saw uniformed baseball players from both teams, and some coaches and umpires listening to a man speaking. The speaker was Chuck Snyder. He was the young married and singles Sunday school teacher at his church. I later discovered Chuck was the chaplain for the Seattle Mariners, and he conducted church services for anyone who wanted to meet on Sundays before the game.

Being naïve, I was under the impression that camaraderie between players from the other team or with umpires before the game might lend oneself to believing that some form of collusion was taking place.

I began to gain an understanding that professional sports are a brotherhood until the first contact takes place during the contest. At that point all brotherhood is separated until the final play of the game. I watched this strange interaction with fascination during batting practice. Players from the opposite teams would be playing catch while others were having casual conversation as they stood around waiting to take turns during batting practice. It was a carnival atmosphere. Steve Largent of the Seattle Seahawks told me, "Professional sports are entertainment, and that is all it is." Each athlete, coach, umpire, media and groundskeeper had one purpose: entertain the fans. I suppose he was right.

Toronto Blue Jay's Player Spit On My Shoe

There is a lot of downtime in major league baseball. It's during those downtimes major league baseball players indulge in activities of personal interest or search for something to do to pass the time until duty calls. The downtimes can be just as taxing on groundskeepers.

It was during the moments prior to the official start of a game between the Toranto Blue Jays and the Seattle Mainers when downtime caught up with a rookie. He had just been brought up from the minor leagues for his first opportunity in the major leagues. It was during this time he let his emotions get the better of him. This ballplayer was engaged in a game of cribbage behind the dugout.

The two ballplayers sat on buckets with a cribbage board sitting on a third bucket between them. It was a heated contest of wills, pride and competition. Several other ballplayers and groundskeepers were watching and badgering the two players as to which card they should play. The rookie was not going to let the veteran players get the best of him. The more they harassed him, the more arrogant and fidgety he became. He was chewing tobacco and increased his chewing as the bantering went on.

In a moment and without warning the rookie ballplayer spit on my shoe. Everyone became quiet recognizing he had stepped over the line of decency. He had not only lost his composure, but defiled another human being. Recognizing his mistake he looked up at me with shock on his face. I'm not sure if he thought he had spit on another player's shoe or it was my Clint Eastwood look of death knocking at his door, but he quickly reached down with his bare hand, wiped the spittle off my shoe, apologized and surprisingly wiped the tobacco on the thigh of his clean uniform. The cribbage game came to an abrupt end and everyone disbursed to their duties as the game was about to begin.

Bird Gets Cat - Cleveland Fans are outraged

BIRD GETS CAT was the headline to the following day's sports page. Nicknames are common in the sports world and Bird was the name of one of our groundskeepers. Bird was working the Seattle Mariner's bullpen when all of a sudden the home plate umpire abruptly stopped the game. He had noticed something no other umpire could see as they were all facing home plate. What he noticed was one of the street cats that lived in the Kingdome had wandered into right field.

Steven Henderson was playing right field. Groundskeeper Bird jumped into action and ran onto the field to retrieve the cat which was now circling Henderson. Not sure how to pick up the cat, he asked Henderson if he could use his glove. Shocked that Bird would make such a request, Henderson declined.

Bird and the cat circled Henderson until Bird made his move. Pouncing into a crouched position, Bird had the cat or the cat had Bird. The cat sank its fangs deep into Bird's hand and began to claw. Bleeding and in pain, Bird threw the cat to the ground. It was during this episode that the camera crew projected the event on the big screen. Now Bird was on center stage and the crowed was beginning to react.

Bird made his final attempt to capture the cat. Thrusting both hands unto the cat and squeezing as hard as he could to insure the cat could not twist around and bite or claw him again Bird carried the cat off the field.

Now getting off the field in the Kingdome from right field was a long walk. The closest exit points were the dugouts. Bird took the cat into the Mariner dugout where an animal cage was waiting for the cat and just outside the Mariner's clubhouse door was an ambulance for Bird. There was concern the street cat might have rabies. Bird spent the night in the hospital and the cat was evaluated for rabies.

Most major league games are broadcast back to the home town and this event was being viewed by fans in Cleveland. The phones began to ring at the Kingdome when the camera crew showed how Seattle fans were reacting as the big screen crew showed close-ups of the action. Cleveland fans were incensed at the inhumane attitude of Seattle fans who were finding humor in the incident and Bird's lack of knowledge in how to properly handle a cat.

The following week the King Country Maintenance Department, who maintained the Kingdome along with the grounds crew, had a mandatory meeting with the Kingdome management, media and the Humane Society.

The meeting started with the usual cursory sharp words of disappointment from management about how we embarrassed the Seattle Mariners and the citizens of Seattle through our lack of concern for small animals. Hence, the meeting was turned over to the Humane Society to show us how to handle animals the humane way.

The Humane Society trainer promptly began by putting a cage on the front table which he said contained a street cat they had just captured. Then he proceeded to open the door and let the cat out. The cat began to wander around the room with all the men dressed in their maintenance gear. Men who were usually rough in language and quick to embarrass each other as they attempted to gain power over their peers suddenly showed signs of concern.

The Humane Society trainer asked if someone would like to demonstrate how to capture this street cat. Several mumbled statements about stepping on it while others lifted their feet when it came by. The trainer allowed the cat to wander throughout the room and under the tables while he demonstrated various capturing devices. I don't think most of the maintenance department or grounds crew listened. They were too busy watching the cat. Finally, the trainer approached the cat, ". . . gently yet firmly grabbing the fur behind the neck and pinning the cat to the floor while at the same moment sliding the other hand under the back legs and gently squeezing." He lifted the cat into the air for all to see and put it back into the cage. The training concluded with everyone signing a letter of apology to the Cleveland Indian organization and the people of Cleveland.

Bird never got rabies, and he never got rid of his nickname.

Four Towels on Towel Night in Exchange for Fours Cuts in the Batting Cage

I was cleaning the Mariner's dugouts several hours before the night's game was to begin. A ballplayer and several coaches were working on the player's hitting mechanics in the batting cage. It was a promotional night and the Mariners were giving away towels to the fans. I had just placed a stack of towels in the Mariner's dugout when one of the coaches yelled, "Hey! Can I have four of those towels?!" Not being one to let an opportunity pass me by, I responded, "Four towels for four cuts in the cage." He said, "Sure", and nodded for me to come over. I gathered up four towels and headed to the batting cage.

When I arrived at the batting cage the coach directed the player to give me his bat. The ballplayer looked at his coach with a startled look. The coach said, "He only wants to take four cuts." The player handed me his bat and asked in an authoritative tone, "Do you know how to hold a bat? It's my game bat." I assured him that I knew how to hit and would not break his bat.

I stepped into the batter's box and focused on the coach who was pitching from behind the pitcher's screen. He was an older gray haired man that appeared to be in fairly good shape for his age. I had watched him pitching to the ballplayer and could see that he threw easy to hit pitches of about 60-70mph. I took a few swings and waited for the first pitch.

The field looked mammoth and the base path looked to be a long way out there. All I could think was, just make solid contact, and don't make a fool of yourself. You know you can never get one over the fence. This was the big leagues and I was going to hit in a big league ball park, with a big league bat, from a big league coach. This was euphoria! How many guys would pay for this opportunity? Yet I was getting paid.

I hit the first three pitches out of the infield. I was elated! Then a coach who had been standing near third base crossed between me and the pitcher. I thought his actions were strange. I was hitting in the cage. It is customary and wise not to pass between the batter and pitcher unless you plan on dodging a hit ball. He made a comment in a derogatory way, "You will never make the big leagues with a swing like that!" Almost before the words left his mouth, the coach who I had given the towels to responded in my defense. "Shut up! He's just having some fun." The rude coach continued his jaunt toward the Blue Jay's dugout. The next pitch I hit in the air into the outfield. I guess he got my adrenalin pumping.

I handed the bat back to the ballplayer and thanked him and the coach for letting me hit. The coach nodded. I walked away not believing what I had been allowed to do. I still have to concentrate to believe I got to hit with a major league team. Dreams can come true.

The Final Four and Playing Basketball on the Main Court

All the members of the grounds crew entered the Kingdome just moments after Georgetown University and Patrick Ewing had won the championship after a decisive victory over the University of Houston. It was our job to dismantle the basketball court's floor from its 4'x 4' x 6" sections of 80 lbs. each. Each section fit like tongue and groove and was numbered. We had to stack 10 sections on pallets. It took two guys to pick up one section and then stack it. Getting them apart was the hard part because you had to finesse each piece while being bent over. Imagine doing this repeatedly from the floor level then lifting the section onto the pallet. After stacking the sections for an hour our backs were super sore and the conversion from a basketball court into a major league baseball field was just getting started.

The media had first priority in the Kingdome. They were always granted as much time as they needed and we had to wait until the last media personnel were out of the playing area before we could start cleaning up. On this particular night one lone media guy was taking forever sending his report. This was pre-computer days. He was manually typing his statement, then sending it electronically. Maybe it was a teletype.

All we could do was was wait for him to finish his report. Someone found a basketball and we started a pick-up game on the main floor. Another dream come true happened for all of us on the grounds crew. Shooting hoops in the Kingdome was surreal. The largest place I had played basketball was in the college gym. You could have put dozens of those gyms in the Kingdome. The glass backboard gave the illusion that the hoop hung freely in space. Not having any depth perception made it very difficult to find the range. Hence, there were many air balls and a lot of chasing the ball. We all got frustrated and gave up trying to play. We decided it was better to just take turns trying to make a hoop while the others retrieved the missed shot.

It was a humbling experience and the defining moment for why I never got to that level of play. My respect for the outside shooters changed after that. Watching shooters hit the three against a glass backboard while fans are waving from behind the glass takes super human concentration.

Pitchers from the Farm Teams Needing Caps from the Concession Stand

During the 1984 baseball season, the Seattle Mariners were getting desperate to find pitchers who could take control of the game. It seemed that every week and sometimes every game new players were being brought up from the minor leagues. Hence, there was a drought on caps in the Mariner's uniform locker.

As the Mariners continued to bring up pitchers the cap supply ran dry. I found that interesting. How could an organization with a huge payroll and expense account not have enough money to buy more caps? Had they not prepared for a need for more caps? The team's equipment manager was buying plastic souvenir caps for the pitchers from the concession stand with an adjustable band. You could tell from anywhere in the Kingdome the pitcher's cap was not the official team cap because of the plastic ventilated top and lighter color. Maybe the cap served as a reminder they had not yet made the major league team.

The word quickly got out to not leave your cap lying around or someone would take it. Some of the rookies tried to trade groundskeepers for their caps, but no one would. Sometimes players from a visiting team would trade for a Mariner's cap, but most didn't because we would have to pay for another one.

Souvenirs – Broken Bats, Balls, Rosin Bag for Cody Webster; 1982 Little League World Champion

One of the cool things about working on the grounds crew was all the memorabilia we had access to. We were allowed to take broken bats, rosin bags, baseballs etc. anything that did not belong to a player. Many times if we knew who the equipment belonged to we would ask them if we could have it. Sometime we could get them to autograph it.

I had the privilege of having Cody Webster, as one of my students. When he was in my seventh grade class, there were school district SLOs – Student Learning Objectives. One of these tests for P.E. was a softball throw. At the time I was 30 years old and Cody was 12. I will never forget watching Cody throw a softball further than I could. It was no wonder the kids from Taiwan could not hit against Cody.

After a Mariner's game I was reorganizing the pitcher's mound and noticed that a rosin bag was left on the mound. It had official labels on it and looked pretty cool. I could not wait to take it to school and give it to Cody.

Sneaking Students into the Kingdome Past Security

One of the crazy things I did during my time with the Seattle Mariners was to sneak a student into the Kingdome. I had a student who was always looking for adventure and took me up on the challenge of sneaking him past security, through the breezeway, through the locker room and under the bleachers. From the shadows of the bleachers he was able to get right next to big league ballplayers.

Although it was not the best example of citizenship or as a role model on my part, I am sure it was a highlight of his junior high years. During those years, when it was permissible for teachers to take students places outside of school hours, I was always looking for cool stuff to do with students.

Sports Illustrated Picture and Gorman Thomas

On an off day for the Mariners, I arrived at work and was greeted with a special assignment. Designated hitter Gorman Thomas was having a photo shoot with Sports Illustrated and it was my job to prepare second base picture perfect. The base had to be freshly painted. No dirt could be on the AstroTurf surrounding the base, and the base area dirt had to be like dust with no large pieces.

I began by sweeping the AstroTurf area around the base to perfection. No dirt was to be visible. Next I painted the base bright white and picture perfect. Then I went about raking the dirt and brooming it to perfection. The final touch was tricky. Carrying the freshly painted base I had to strategically step through the dirt area, set the base in place, and back out on the same steps I made going in. With each backward step I took, I had to bend down and smooth out the previous step being ever so careful not to leave a trace.

Everything was perfect when all of a sudden the second base area lit up as bright as the sun. The whole 200 section had lights spaced at about every 100 feet completely encircling second base.

As I stood there in wonder, two photographers walked up and introduced themselves as photographers for Sports Illustrated, and that they were there to take pictures of Gorman Thomas casting with his fly rod from second base. What, Gorman Thomas casting with his fly rod from second base? Now this was getting interesting. I asked the photographers, "What did fly casting have to do with baseball?" The lead photographer stated, "Sports Illustrated is doing a personal interest story on Gorman Thomas's hobby." The other photographer was on his radio talking to someone on the second level about the lighting.

Moments later Gorman Thomas appeared from the Mariner's dugout in his game uniform carrying his fly rod and taking a few practice casts as he approached our group. The lead photographer instructed Gorman Thomas to place one foot on second base and use the other to stabilize himself, while he took a few casts as they took pictures. My job was to smooth out Gorman Thomas's footprints making the surface he was standing on picture perfect. When a picture was taken all the lights on the 200 level came on in one giant flash illuminating second base. All this fuss with the lighting and base preparation took several hours for a few minutes of photographs. It was amazing to think of how much effort goes into making a magazine article and this was only the photo shoot.

After Gorman Thomas left, the Sports Illustrated guys asked if I would like my picture taken. They didn't need to ask twice. They handed me a baseball as a prop and had me pose on second base while the 200 level lights flashed. They handed me an instamatic picture, signed the back and said thanks.

It was hard to believe that I had been photographed by Sports Illustrated. My picture never made it to an issue of Sports Illustrated, but neither did the Gorman Thomas article.

High School Baseball State Championships and Player Wanting a Glass of Dirt from Second Base

Back in the Kingdome days high school baseball state championship games were held in the Kingdome. On the final day of the games the grounds crew had to get the field ready for the Mariner's game.

I was sitting in the dugout watching the final game. This was a special treat because during a major league game, the closest you could get to sitting in the dugout was on a bucket in the doorway.

As the game came to an end I was assigned to second base for pregame preparations. During my work I heard a desperate voice ask, "Mister? Could I get some of the dirt?" He had a hotel glass that he wished to put some dirt in. I told him it was alright. He acted like it was Christmas, and I guess in a way it was.

Mowing Head of Security's Lawn and Messing Around with Scott on the Gator

The off the field part of the job of grounds crew is the maintaining of the grounds outside of the stadium. This is where the fans don't see you and the excitement of the game is lost. One of those tedious jobs was mowing the head of securities lawn. He was provided a house with an eight foot chain link fence and locking gate next to the downtown train station.

Scott and I jumped into the gator and headed toward the head of security's house to mow his lawn. It was great that the city had provided him a house, but next door to the train station? I was driving and Scott was entertaining himself with a baseball he found along the way. Scott was throwing the ball into the air and catching it as we moved along. Scott began to wonder about the physics of us moving forward and whether the ball when tossed up would stay with us or if we would be moving faster. Scott began to toss the ball higher and higher with each toss estimating the rate of the ball's descent and speed of the gator.

Scott was just beginning to get the height of the toss and our speed figured out when I got an idea. What if I swerved quickly just as he tossed the ball? Obviously the ball would not return to Scott, but would Scott attempt to grab it. His concentration was high, and I was concerned about him being so intense with his experiment that he might actually jump from the gator and land on the parking lot. I thought he might get hurt, but it was worth finding out. Scott tossed the ball and I swerved to the left. Scott's body almost left the gator and he quickly grabbed the gator, forgetting about the ball. Needless to say Scott was not happy. We turned around and retrieved the baseball.

Mowing the yard was a one-man job which we usually took turns doing. Scott was the senior member of our duo and he had paved the way for me to get a groundkeeper job, so as my reward for messing with his physics experiment I mowed the lawn by myself while Scott sat relaxing in the gator.

Players Playing Catch and Getting Hit

The job of a groundskeeper can be hazardous and you must be paying attention at all times even during pregame activities. Ever wonder when ballplayers practice? Prior to every game, players take batting practice, field hit balls, play catch, work on skills and sometimes mess around. It's during the messing around times groundskeepers need to pay extra close attention.

Ballplayers loosen up their arms and work on their catching and throwing skills in long lines.

It seems that since these athletes have been doing this since they were young, it should be routine to catch a ball. One would think that walking behind these lines would be safe.

I can be naïve at times believing we live in a world of responsible people where individuals make wise choices and avoid foolish actions. I have since come to believe my thinking is flawed. I now believe most people are self-centered and often don't consider others in their actions, hence it is wise to keep your eye on the other guy or you could be victimized and blamed for not knowing better.

While walking behind a throwing line, I heard a slap sound and felt a sharp pain in my upper thigh. It didn't take but a second to realize I had been hit by a thrown ball. Sure enough there lay the ball that hit my leg. As a ballplayer said, "You must excuse him. He has a terrible curve ball." I responded, "You are a professional and are supposed to catch it." He did not respond and went back to playing catch.

Note to self: Make sure to not walk behind throwing lines again. It can be dangerous to your health.

This Week in Baseball - Highlight Film

Sitting in the bullpen had its dangers. The bullpens were located just outside of the playing areas of right and left fields, hence any ball hit foul had the potential of flying right into those sitting on the bench. There was no barrier. You were constantly a target and needed to be paying close attention to what was going on. A foul ball being chased down by a player meant you had better get out of their way. A line drive toward the bullpen was often hard to judge because of the angle and how fast it was coming. A fellow groundskeeper and I were humiliated as we learned this lesson.

We were sitting on the far end of the Mariner's bullpen bench. Greg, the other groundskeeper, was sitting to my left when the batter hit a line drive toward the Mariner's bullpen. The ball was tailing toward where we had been sitting because we were now standing, expecting to be out of the way. The ball was rapidly coming our way, so I pushed Greg telling him to run down the wall. Greg began to run. I was using him as a shield and had my hand on his back. In case he made a sudden move I wanted him to stay in front of me. It turned out that we were actually running into the path of the speeding ball. Greg began to stop but I kept yelling "run" when I heard a smack and a groan. Greg was hit by the ball in the thigh. We found our way back to the bullpen with Greg limping and scolding me for telling him to run.

As we sat in the bullpen with the Mariner's relief pitchers and coaches laughing at us, Greg let me know in clear language that he did not want to be on This Week in Baseball's highlight film. Well we were. Everyone laughed except Greg.

Boredom in the Bullpen

Relief pitchers can wait days before they get called to pitch, but every day they must suit up for the game and wait for the phone in the bullpen to ring calling for a pitcher. So what do they do to spend their time?

I have been asked by relief pitchers what the banners meant that circled the stadium's 200 level, where the best place to eat was, and engaged in conversations about being a school teacher and groundskeeper. I have seen pitchers doing Sudoku puzzles, crossword puzzles, going through their various pitches with a weighted ball, trying to scare groundskeepers with strange almost demented comments to make them think they are crazy, and putting matches between a sleeping pitchers sock and their shoes, then lighting it and waiting until it burned down far enough to burn the sleeping guy's foot.

One night in particular one of the pitchers had brought a squeeze toy. It had an air bulb with a tube that connected to legs. When they squeezed the bulb the legs shot out.

Makes me wonder about the emotional levels the pitchers go through from being totally bored to when the phone rings and they're on center stage and focused.

Kids Hiding Behind the Left Field Wall

Show me a youngster that doesn't want to play on a major league field and I'll show you a youngster that doesn't appreciate America's greatest pastime.

At the end of each game in the Kingdome, the lights were turned down low. The purpose was to encourage fans to leave the stadium. I once saw the lights turned down just as the winning run baserunner touched home plate. It was like there was a switch on the plate.

One night the groundskeepers were sitting in the visitor's dugout waiting to prepare the field for the next day's game. Little did we know that a group of youngsters had been planning to hide behind the left field fence, and when the lights were turned down they would emerge from the fence and begin a game of pop-up. A bat, one ball and everyone with a glove in hand got into the game right away. In the dim light of the Kingdome we watched this event unfold. It was like watching the movie *Field of Dreams*.

It was about 400 feet to where the youngster eagerly played. After all, our work was on the infield, so why not let them have some fun? I could only imagine them wondering how long they could play before being escorted from the stadium or worse, the police might show up. None of us were eager to chase them away. I think we understood their passion for the sport and were probably envious of their youthful bravery.

After several minutes, we started our work on the infield pretending to ignore the young ball players in left field. My eye caught movement from my right. It was Wilber, our grounds crew leader on the gator. He was slowly making his way toward the pop-up game. Once the youngsters saw Wilber they quickly exited the field and vanished through the left field fence as if they were entering a fourth dimension. To this day I am baffled as to how they got through the twenty foot fence. I had helped put the fence up several times and know that it was designed to keep players and baseballs safely in the field of play.

Having worked with teenagers for 37 years in public education and juvenile detention centers, this is one of the many things they have taught me – youngsters can get into and out of anything. Combine the love for baseball with a blend of adventure, they experience youth as it was meant to be, enjoying their passion for life and baseball on their field of dreams.

Umpire Takes Foul Tip in the Throat

It could be said that being an umpire is a thankless job. In the early days of baseball the umpire was fair game for criticism, harassment and sometimes abuse to the point of being pummeled by fans and ballplayers to the point of death. It wasn't until the owners of the early teams realized that the game was in jeopardy of losing its respect and control due to the lack of individuals willing to umpire games. When stronger guidelines and protections were offered to the umpires, a sense of control began to emerge.

Being an umpire behind the plate has its own hazards. I have met umpires who have received broken arms, legs and concussions from foul tips.

I was sitting in the dugout door when the game came to a sudden stop as the home plate umpire made his way to the dugout. He was holding his throat with the team trainer and the other umpires following. As he came through the door it was obvious he was in great pain. He was having trouble breathing and his wind pipe was red. A foul tip had hit him in the throat. I had never before nor since seen a baseball game stopped because the entire umpire staff had left the field. The players just stood around looking at each other. Some were visiting with a baserunner while the batter and catcher had a chat. It was very interesting to see that without someone to keep order of the game, there was no game. I also learned that there were backup umpires on hand if something like this happened. After a few minutes and a thorough check up by the trainers the home plate umpire decided to return to the game. He entered the stadium to the applause to the fans.

Shortly after this event and many others like it, a plastic shield was hung from the bottom of the face mask to protect the throat. Later the actual face mask was extended to replace the cumbersome plastic shield. Eventually many catchers began wearing a hockey goalie type mask to avoid injury.

Duty in the assignment behind the plate can be dangerous for all those subjecting themselves to be targets of a speeding ball. I wonder how long it took before catchers and umpires began to wear any protective equipment at all. The first ones wore none.

Umpires Leftover Dinners

Another change major league baseball umpires have experienced is getting a nice meal. The meal was usually served prior to the game in the umpire's dressing room. Most nights the umpires would not eat the meal. I later learned the umpires found it easier to stay focused on an empty stomach. When the game was over their adrenalin level was so high they were not hungry. The umpires would shower and exit the stadium looking for a place to eat and relax with the umpire crew. This meant the umpires' meal was offered to the grounds crew who had been sitting and watching the game for three hours and were plenty hungry.

The umpires' meals were brought to the grounds crew who could eat in the dugout before starting their nightly duties of preparing the field for the next game. Those full course meals were pretty good and came from the stadium chef.

Club House Food if Visiting Team Lost

Food was always a good reason to root for the Mariners. You see if the visiting team lost the team would exit the stadium as quickly as possible. Sometimes the visiting clubhouse manager would invite the grounds crew into the clubhouse to eat what the ballplayers had left.

Every now and then you could get a glimpse of a ball player who was one of the last ones out of the club house, but the rules were strictly enforced – don't talk to or about the players when in the clubhouse. The clubhouse was their sanctuary. It was their home away from home.

The most interesting part of going into the clubhouse was seeing the names on the lockers of the players most people only see on TV. The groundskeepers would probably never play in the major leagues, but it was as close as you could get without actually being in a game. Fans would pay money to experience what we did, yet we got paid. I'm also sure that most of us would have done the job for free just to be around the ballplayers and be part of the big show.

Cleaning the Big Screen

Have you ever wondered how the big screen at the stadium gets cleaned? I hadn't and quite frankly I didn't think about it. It just didn't occur to me. I, like most people, take it for granted and just enjoy watching the action on the big screen.

I entered the stadium on a nongame day expecting to have another day of preparing the bullpens, base paths, batting area and pitcher's mound. As I came closer to the stadium floor, I noticed a gigantic crane in left field. The crane's arm was extended over one hundred feet to the big screen where a guy in a bucket was using what looked to be a giant squeegee on a thirty foot pole. He was cleaning the big screen one pass at a time. I could only think, "That is going to take forever."

The big screen was like a giant computer monitor. Being an electronic device, it attracted dust particles which stuck to the screen. It was really interesting to see how much more clear the picture was after cleaning.

I'm not sure how they clean the screens these days, but if it's the same as during that time period my respect goes to the guy suspended in a bucket several hundred feet above the seats.

Food Poisoned Ball Girl

One of the prized jobs in the Kingdome was being a ball girl for the Marines.   Being close to the action, fans and ball players was special until one night.

The ball girl sat on her stool patiently waiting to intercept any foul ball that found its way toward the bullpen.   It was her job to keep the bullpen catcher from being hit in the back by a foul ball. The bullpen catcher was the only member of the team whose back was to the batter, not a good situation even if the catcher was approximately 100 yards from home plate.

Ball girls were the darlings of the game. Everyone got excited when a ball was hit in their vicinity. Some of the girls had very good skills and made some spectacular catches.   Often the girl would give the ball to a young fan and engage in friendly conversation with fans between innings.

Throughout this particular game, I noticed that one of the ball girls, who was usually quite animated and engaging with the fans did not appear to be moving very well and was not having her usual fun. As the night wore on I noticed after one of the innings the ball girl walking toward the dugout. It was unusual for a ball girl to leave her post during the game. A few minutes later a different girl replaced the ball girl. As usual, the bullpen pitchers were curious and had to know what had happened to the other ball girl. To the dismay of the pitcher, who had been sent on the mission of finding out what happened, the replacement ball girls had no information for him.

As the game came to an end, I found myself behind the Mariner's dugout preparing for the postgame duties. As I passed through the dugout door I was greeted by a group of medical personnel and the ball girl laying on a gurney. She appeared to be her joyful self and was very talkative. She was pleading with anyone who would listen to call her mom and tell her not to eat the chicken in the refrigerator. She informed us that she and her mother had bought some chicken for lunch. They had taken the chicken to one of the city's popular lakes to eat and then walked around the lake. The chicken they had not finished eating was left on the car seat in the hot sun. She had driven separately in order to get ready for the night's game. The ball girl took the chicken home and ate a little more before she left. She was so impressed with the amazing taste she left a note on the refrigerator door encouraging her mom to try some.

I wonder if they both ended up in the hospital, possibly sharing the same room.

Big League Wannabe Girl Asked for a Tryout with the Yankees

As I approached the Kingdome, I could not help but notice a young woman throwing a baseball against the wall. I had seen her before and thought nothing of it. She had decent mechanics, could hit her target and threw hard. I figured she was passing time until the gates opened. I learned of her intentions when she appeared behind the Yankees bullpen.

Many youngsters live the dream of becoming a big league ballplayer. I saw it all the time at the Kingdome. It's been said, "Everyone becomes a kid at the ballpark." I think that is true. People get caught up in the game and all the fanfare that takes place. It's almost a magical experience for those enamored with the sport.

One season the Seattle Mariners had a batting contest between fans during the 7th inning stretch. Three fans' names were chosen to compete in hitting three baseballs. The object was to select the longest hit ball from the three contestants and that person got to advance to the next round until the championship round later in the season. The winner won a prize from the Mariner Baseball Organization.

One night a tall and very strong twenty-something young man took his swings. Both dugouts were lined with the ballplayers waiting to see how this fan was going to do. He hit the first ball into the one hundred level seats about five rows over the left field wall. The next hit went a little further. The ballplayers began to get excited and were making comments about his strength and joking that some of their fellow teammates might be looking for a new job if the scouts invited this fan for a tryout. His final hit was way over the wall in centerfield. The ball players laughed and shook their heads.

During another fan competition, fans were given a gigantic glove. They were supposed to catch a fly ball with it. Each fan was given three fly balls to attempt catching just one.

Well you can imagine what some fans thought when they had the chance to go on the field, hit, catch, and run the bases. For some fans reality became a fantasy that they were really good enough to play in the big leagues, and so it was with the young woman who threw the ball against the Kingdome wall.

I was assigned to sit in the Yankee's bullpen on this particular night. When I approached the bullpen, I noticed the same young woman hanging over the railing with her glove and baseball in hand. As the game progressed she became more vocal and bolder as she engaged in conversation with the bullpen players. She told them about her ability to throw various pitches and hoped to play in the big leagues someday. At first the players were friendly and encouraged her to find a team to play on, but she had another agenda. Further into the game she began to figure out who the coaches were, and they became the focus of her conversation. When they lost interest and turned their focus to the job of coaching, the young woman turned once again to talking with the players.

During the 7th inning stretch, she asked one of the players if she could get a tryout. Bullpen pitchers are always looking for something creative to do with their down time, so this request presented them with the perfect opportunity for entertainment. When she kept prodding to the point of begging for a tryout, the pitchers informed her that they had no control over tryouts, but if she asked one of the coaches they might agree. The bullpen pitchers had a good laugh as the coaches systematically were approached for a tryout. After the coaches stopped speaking to the young woman she realized that her efforts were in vain.

It's a harsh reality that the majority of youngsters have a dream to play in the big leagues, yet fail to have the skills necessary to play at that level. I have seen many young boys and girls play really good baseball. Our son had a friend whose sister was the starting pitcher on her middle school baseball team. She was that good, but good is not great.

When reality becomes a fantasy feelings get hurt.

Sliding Powder and Spike Owen's Torn Pants

Hanging around major league sports is an education all of its own. The sport does not matter because each sport has its own life and experiences. I was able to be a part of various professional sports events during my time at the Kingdome and learned special elements that were specific to each sport.

One particular event allowed me to understand major league baseball from a different perspective. You see there are several products which make the game of baseball easier and safer to conduct. One of those products is called Diamond Dust. We never had to use Diamond Dust in the Kingdome because it is used to absorb water. Although it rains in Seattle, we had the enclosed Kingdome. As a side note, when much discussion was being had about the new Safeco Field and whether or not it should have a fixed roof, a particular piece of research was interesting. Someone did a study on Mariner's games canceled or delayed due to rain. The study revealed that the Mariners had more away games impacted by rain than home games had been. Hence, Safeco Field has a retractable roof, but I digress. Diamond Dust is typically used on pitching mounds. The purpose is to provide for better grip for the pitcher when they come down on their forward foot making their delivery safer and reducing the chance of slipping or injury. On the other hand Sliding Powder improves sliding, and Sliding Powder was the focus for Spike Owens during this particular game.

Spike was coming in hot to second base and needed to slide to avoid the tag. I could not believe what I saw. Spike took flight and lunged toward second base with a feet first slide attempting to steal. You see Spike simply stuck where he was when he started his slide. He did slide a little and then stopped about two feet from the bag. The shortstop had to reach down and tag Spike who was not where the shortstop thought he would be.

Spike got up showing some pain which was causing some concern with the trainer, teammates and coaching staff. I was located in the Mariner's dugout door wondering what caused Spike to stop sliding. Well it didn't take long to find out what Spike thought. As he walked through the dugout door with the trainer in tow, it was obvious he was not happy. He was looking at a tear in his pants which revealed an abrasion on his buttocks which was oozing some blood. The first thing he said to Wilber, the head groundskeeper, and me was, "Don't you guys have sliding powder!?" After Spike entered the clubhouse and nobody was around, I looked at Wilber and asked, "What's 'sliding powder'?" Wilber sheepishly looked at me and said, "Something we don't have." I'm sure Wilber put "sliding powder" on his list of supplies.

Alvin Davis's Injuries Escalated

Major league athletes realize they can be replaced at any time and injuries can get in the way of a long career. A replacement player can do a stellar job and sometimes take the place of the regular starter. Hence, athletes will attempt to hide an injury hoping to recover before the injury makes a major impact on their performance. Major league athletes are gifted in more than one set of skills. Most of them can play several sports at a level most of us only dream of achieving. If they become injured, they are able to call upon another set of muscles and nerves that still surpass a good athlete. The major league athlete is not in the good or even best category of most athletes. They are in a class all their own. They are phenoms.

Alvin Davis was one of those athletes. Alvin never understood words like maybe, quit, can't, or I'll do better next time. Alvin Davis put his best forward every time. When he was injured, he could still outplay most athletes at the major league baseball level.

Major league baseball does not allow downtime for recovery from injuries, if you are going to stay in the major league. They might be placed on the disabled list and be moved to one of the organization's minor league teams until they are again able to perform at the major league level. Some never return even after recovery from an injury, and Alvin Davis knew this. He had fought hard to achieve a starting position with the Seattle

Mariners and was not going to take the chance of being sent to a minor league team again.

At the close of the game, I was cleaning the Mariner's dugout and needed to get supplies from the Mariner's clubhouse. Something caught my eye in the training room, it was Alvin Davis sitting on the trainer's table with his arm and leg packed in ice with stimulating electrodes to help with his muscle injuries. He was a mess! During the game I didn't notice Alvin's performance being limited. I did notice that he did not lunge toward first base when he was running and he seemed a little slow, but that is seen often when a runner knows he cannot beat the throw.

Apparently in an earlier game, Alvin had pulled a hamstring when lunging for first base. It was not obvious or he would have been pulled from the starting line-up. Because Alvin was playing first base and not required to make long throws, he began to rely solely on his arm. He was protecting his leg and hoping it would heal. Using his upper body only and not pushing off with his leg required him to twist his back in an unnatural motion. That motion began to impact his back.

Alvin Davis was a major league baseball player of the caliber I mentioned above. Even with a torn hamstring and sore shoulder, he was able to draw upon the strength of his back and still perform at a major league level. His natural gifts of throwing, hitting and running were far superior to the best baseball players which caused him to find ways to use his injured body to perform at a professional level even when injured.

Although Alvin Davis did go on the disabled list, he did not lose his starting position and went on to play several more years and received MVP honors several times as a major league baseball player.

Final Words

Major League sports are one of life's great teachers about how to be determined and self-disciplined. I gained a new perspective about Major League Baseball when working with the Seattle Mariners.

The 1984-1985 seasons came at just the right time in my life, as most dreams do. Those years contain very special memories which I have attempted to share in this small memoir.

I hope you get the chance to experience what I did by talking to your local major league stadium management office. You too can catch your dream.

Contact Rich at -

korbri@gmail.com

Made in the USA
Coppell, TX
08 April 2023